# What other Scripture Journey participants have to say...

*"Just as soaking up the sun can give you a healthy tan (and much needed Vitamin D!), soaking up God's truth gives us healthy minds and hearts. It's a spiritual bath to understand the arc of each book of the Bible, but then dive deep to revel in the particulars. I love the way Keith guides us into the light and warmth of God's truth."*

Gary Thomas (Speaker and Best-Selling Author of *Sacred Marriage* and *Authentic Faith*)

*"Has your Bible reading time become stale, aimless, and scattered? God can use the Scripture Journey series to not only transform your understanding of the Bible, but far more importantly, to draw you into a more personal relationship with God. Now is the perfect time to discover a fresh, consistent and deeper approach to spending time with God through His Word! Take this journey. You won't regret it."*

Dr. Rob Rienow (Co-Founder, Visionary Family Ministries)

*"Approaching eight decades, I have used many Bible study plans. But Keith Ferrin's approach to saturate your mind and spirit with Scripture is simplicity at its best!"*

Judith Maxwell

*"I highly recommend Keith's Bible studies for both group and personal study. Looking at the whole book to get the big picture before focusing on the individual parts and details gives a completely different perspective. In addition, looking at verses in context helps give a more accurate understanding."*

Serene Mendicino

*"I loved the Scripture Journey. Opened my eyes to truths I have not seen before."*

Jim Jacobs

*"I really enjoy studying the Bible this way! We read, re-read, and really absorbed the whole book before digging into the details. It helped me get a glimpse of God's bigger picture. Plus, when we shifted to looking at the details, what I learned stuck with me so much more, since I had laid such a good foundation. Thank you, Keith!"*

Tanya Quakenbush

*"Reading the Bible was something I felt I 'had' to do as a Christian, but it did not come alive as God's Word to me until I started reading it with a relational mindset. Now, every day, I am excited to see what God is going to say to me, even if I have read the same words 100 times. This approach changed my life!"*

Vicki Berg

*"I am loving the studies in the Scripture Journey Series. Each one allows me to go back in time with the Holy Spirit-inspired writers of the Scriptures. Paul's life in particular, and his personal walk with the Lord has helped me develop a more intimate relationship with Jesus, my Savior and with God the Father and with the Holy Spirit. I now enjoy my own personal journey into the pages of the Bible more than ever."*

Sheri Green

# Gospel of John Scripture Journey

## A 40-Day Bible Study Through the Gospel of John

**Keith Ferrin**

Keith Ferrin Productions, LLC

Published by Keith Ferrin Productions, LLC



Back cover photo: Scott Yamamura, Created to Create, Seattle, WA

Cover Design: Robert Calvin Williams III, www.ilovemycover.com

ISBN: 9798884977587



For information or to schedule author appearances:

Keith Ferrin

www.keithferrin.com

keith@keithferrin.com

# Dedication

This book is dedicated to Bruce Kuhn. If I hadn't seen your presentation of the *Gospel of Luke* – and spent nine hours with you the next day – I wouldn't have internalized the *Gospel of John*. Your presentation transformed the way I read, ponder, and teach the Word.

I am forever grateful.
Keith

# Contents

# Introduction

Ever since 1994, the year I spent reading and internalizing the *Gospel of John*, this book has been "home" for me. I can't wait for you to start, or continue, your journey with this remarkable gospel.

The *Gospel of John* is filled with miracles, teachings, conversations, prayers, death, resurrection, and relationships. All from the perspective of John, one of the twelve disciples, who refers to himself simply as "*the one whom Jesus loved.*"

As John approached the end of his writing, he penned these words as his *reason* for writing:

> *"Jesus performed many other signs in the presence of His disciples, which are not written in this book. But these are written so that you may believe that Jesus is the Christ, the Son of God, and that by believing you may have life in His name."* (John 20:30-31)

The daily thoughts and guidance on the following pages are intentionally brief. The reason is so that you will spend less time reading *my* book and more time reading *His Book.* Even more simply, my prayer is that you would spend more time with the Author. With Jesus. Grasping the Father's heart for you a little bit more each day. Guided by the Holy Spirit through each encounter.

After all, it is only through the Father, the Son, and the Holy Spirit that you will discover life. Real life. Eternal life.

Grab your Bible and join me for the *Gospel of John Scripture Journey.*

Alongside,

# How to Use This Book

As I wrote the *Gospel of John Scripture Journey* (and each of the Bible studies in the *Scripture Journey Series*), my goal was always to make this both helpful and easy-to-use for individuals, families, small groups or Sunday School classes, or any group gathering to read and discuss God's Word.

## For Individuals

Each day you will find guidance on what to read in your Bible. I don't print the actual passages in this book because part of going on a *Scripture Journey* is being in your Bible!

After the daily Bible reading, you will find a section called *For Reflection & Discussion.* In this section you will find questions, thoughts to ponder, or ideas for digging deeper.

Finally, at the end of each day I have a page for *Notes & Prayers.* Some Scripture journey-goers find this page helpful for jotting down ideas, thoughts, prayers, or even words or themes you want to explore more deeply after completing the *Gospel of John Scripture Journey.* Others choose to use a separate journal or digital notebook (especially if you're reading a digital version rather than the physical book) for more thorough reflection, note-taking, or journaling.

One Recommendation: While using the *Gospel of John Scripture Journey* as an individual is certainly beneficial, to get the most out of the journey – and have more fun doing it! – I highly recommend finding at least one friend to discuss what you are discovering.

## For Families

I love doing *Scripture Journeys* with my wife and kids! Depending on the ages of your children, you might need to adjust the *For Reflection & Discussion* section. Add some extra questions, leave some questions out, or put them in your own words. After all, you know your kids way better than I do!

You might also want to decide ahead of time what a realistic timeframe is for your family to go on the *Gospel of John Scripture Journey*. You will notice that I laid it out for 40 days. I have intentionally left out any spaces for dates, weeks, or months.

If your family reads the Bible together every day...terrific! Make it 40 days. If five days each week is more realistic with your current schedule, tell your kids you're going on an 8-Week Scripture Journey. Three or four days each week can be a 10-Week or 12-Week Scripture Journey. These last few options leave the weekends for "catching up" if you need to!

Remember...This is *relational* time. It is not just about learning something or "getting through" the daily reading. God's desire – and design – is for us to be in relationship. Relationship with Him. Relationship with each other.

## For Small Groups and Sunday School Classes

While some small group studies (or classes) are designed in a way that participants don't need to do much during the week, that is not the case for the *Gospel of John Scripture Journey*. The discussion is only going to flow if participants are spending time during the week "traveling alone" on the journey, with the small group or class time as a place for discussing what each person noticed on their journey.

That said, I encourage you to talk through this at the beginning and agree on how long the journey will be. As with families, this can be 40 days or 8, 10, or 12 weeks. From past *Scripture Journeys* I have done with groups, I have found the best experiences are either an 8-Week or 10-Week journey. (Four or five days of reading each week.)

Since the *For Reflection & Discussion* section is printed right in the book, there is no need for a "leader's guide" or "participant's guide." Each person has the same book. (I like simple!)

# Day 1

Welcome to Day 1 of the *Gospel of John Scripture Journey*! This is going to be amazing! (It's also going to be encouraging, challenging, inspiring, eye-opening, and a bunch of other adjectives. The *Gospel of John* is just *that good!*)

Before diving in, I want to give you a bit of a "roadmap" for the journey ahead. You can think of these 40 days like a Broadway play. You can watch the whole play. You can see how it's broken down into "acts." And each act is broken down into "scenes."

The first 10 days we will simply read the *Gospel of John*. (Watch the "play" and discover the "acts.")

Days 16-35 we will explore a selection of verses. (Dive into each "scene" of the *Gospel of John*.)

Days 36-40 we will re-watch the "play" another time or two.

Ok. Enough setup. Are you ready to begin the *Gospel of John Scripture Journey*? For today...it is really complicated. (wink)

## Today's Passage: Read the *Gospel of John* for 20-30 minutes.

Yup...that's it. Simply read. Obviously, you're not reading the entire book each day. The goal is to read through the *Gospel of John* at least two times – or more if you are able! – before Day 11. This is "Big Picture" time. Not "Study Deeply" time. We'll get to that soon enough!

Pray before you begin, asking – and expecting – God to meet you as you read His Word. Read the *Gospel of John* in a *physical Bible*. Why a physical Bible? It's all about distractions vs. focus. I am not against digital Bibles. Having a Bible app on your phone or tablet can be a wonderful resource. But not as your *main* Bible. Here is my reasoning in a nutshell.

> *"Few things are more distracting than holding something in your hand that can do 1,000 things. Few things will help you focus more than holding something that can only do one."*

Ready? Set? Read!

## For Reflection & Discussion

- What are your first impressions?
- What hopes do you have for this journey?
- Spend some time asking God to guide you on the journey, as well as bring His Word to your mind throughout each day (not only when you are reading).

# Notes & Prayers

# Day 2

**Today's Passage: Read the *Gospel of John* for 20-30 minutes.**

This first week or two, each day is going to be somewhat similar. **Remember: We're watching the play.** Grasping the storyline. Building a foundation. Laying the groundwork. This is the time for you to leave the notes, study Bibles, and commentaries aside. (We will pick them up soon enough.)

Simply read. You and your Heavenly Father. Let Him remind you of His truths, His presence, and His hope for you today.

## For Reflection & Discussion

- For the next several days, the questions are going to be the same. This is our first walk through the *Gospel of John*. You want to train yourself to read with your eyes, heart, and mind wide open to what God has for you.
- What stood out to you today as you read?
- What encouraged or challenged you?
- What confused you?
- What person or event are you looking forward to exploring more deeply?

## Notes & Prayers

# Day 3

**Today's Passage: Read the *Gospel of John* for 20-30 minutes.**

During these first 10 days, we're "watching the play." As you do, especially during your second and third times reading the *Gospel of John,* you can also look at the "acts." There are a couple ways to view the "acts" contained in the *Gospel of John.*

Notice the natural breaks. Not between individual events, but in between *major time periods.* You can have as few or many "acts" as you'd like. Look for time periods like the "early weeks" of ministry, or the "miracles and teaching of Jesus," or "Passion Week."

Passion Week (a.k.a "Holy Week") refers to the final week of Jesus' life leading up to his crucifixion and resurrection. It begins with Jesus's "Triumphal Entry" (Chapter 12) into Jerusalem on Palm Sunday. Passion Week ends with Jesus's resurrection on Easter. (Chapter 20) John spends almost half of his gospel covering this one week, so you might want to divide this time period into a few smaller periods.

Another way to look at the "acts" in the *Gospel of John*, is to have each "act" be one of the *major themes* of the book. While John covers many topics and themes, he keeps returning to these five primary themes:

1. The Divinity of Jesus

2. Light vs. Darkness

3. The Importance of Belief and Faith

4. Love and Redemption

5. Eternal Life and Resurrection

You might even want to jot these five themes in a journal or notebook and add events, conversations, and Scripture references (chapters and verses) so you can look at these themes more deeply on a weekend, or after you've completed the *Gospel of John Scripture Journey*.

## For Reflection & Discussion

- What stood out to you today as you read?
- What encouraged or challenged you?
- What confused you?
- What person or event are you looking forward to exploring more deeply?

## Notes & Prayers

# Day 4

**Today's Passage: Read the *Gospel of John* for 20-30 minutes.**

As you read today, let me encourage you to read out loud. Stick with your physical Bible, but add your voice to your reading.

You might be wondering why I am encouraging you to read out loud. It's quite simple. When we read out loud, we naturally read with more emotion. Reading with more emotion makes it easier to focus, not to mention it makes our reading more fun. Finally, we also remember what we both see and hear significantly more than what we *only* see or *only* hear.

Many people feel strange reading the Bible out loud to themselves. However, most people who stick with it for a week or two find it so beneficial for focus and retention, they end up reading the Bible out loud the rest of their lives!

## For Reflection & Discussion

- Did you notice anything different as you read out loud?
- What stood out to you today as you read?
- What encouraged or challenged you?
- What confused you?
- What person or event are you looking forward to exploring more deeply?

## Notes & Prayers

# Day 5

**Today's Passage: Read the *Gospel of John* for 20-30 minutes and do an *Author* background study.**

Almost any Bible teacher will tell you, "*Context is key.*" Throughout these first ten days, I would encourage you to do three different Background Studies:

- The Author – Who wrote the book?
- The Audience – To whom was the book written?
- The Atmosphere – What was happening at that time (in the culture, for the author, and for the audience)?

For some people, Background Studies will become a bit of a hobby. I know people who spend hours reading, researching, and discovering all kinds of interesting background information. If that's you...wonderful! If not...even 10-15 minutes spent discovering a bit more about the context will make your reading richer and more fruitful.

I often think of it like going to a live concert where the musician tells you "The story behind the song." Knowing where the song came from changes the way you listen to it for years to come. The same is true with the Bible.

If you own a study Bible, there is probably some background info in there about John. If you don't, you can go to a free Bible study site – like BibleHub or BlueLetter Bible – and find out more about him.

You can also ask a friend or pastor what resources they recommend.

## For Reflection & Discussion

- What is one thing you learned about John from your research you didn't already know?
- What stood out to you today as you read?
- What encouraged or challenged you?
- What confused you?
- What person or event are you looking forward to exploring more deeply?

## Notes & Prayers

# Day 6

**Today's Passage: Read the *Gospel of John* for 20-30 minutes.**

Since the *Gospel of John* takes about two hours to read, there's a good chance that today (or yesterday or tomorrow) you'll be starting your second trip through the book. You might consider reading it in a different translation this time.

If you own a physical Bible in a different translation than your primary one...grab it. If not, open up the YouVersion Bible app or www.BibleGateway.com and you'll find plenty of translations to choose from.

Here are the ones I personally like to read throughout the first few weeks: (Choose a few.)

Christian Standard Bible

New Living Translation

Berean Standard Bible

English Standard Version

New International Version

King James Version (or the New King James Version)

The Message (This is a paraphrase, rather than a translation)

## For Reflection & Discussion

- What stood out to you today as you read?
- What encouraged or challenged you?
- What confused you?
- What person or event are you looking forward to exploring more deeply?

## Notes & Prayers

# Day 7

**Today's Passage: Read the *Gospel of John* for 20-30 minutes.**

The main goal for these first ten days (whether you're doing ten in a row or 4-5 days each week) is to read through the *Gospel of John* at least twice before you get to *Day 11*. If you are still in your first reading, take a look at your calendar and see if there is a day in the next week when you could block out a little extra time.

If not, is there a way to add 5-10 minutes to the daily reading you're already doing? Could you add a second "reading slot" in your day? For example, if you've been reading for 20 minutes or so in the mornings, could you take 10 minutes of your lunch break – or the last 10 minutes before you turn the lights off at night – to read a little more?

## For Reflection & Discussion

- What stood out to you today as you read?
- What encouraged or challenged you?
- What confused you?
- What person or event are you looking forward to exploring more deeply?

## Notes & Prayers

# DAY 8

**Today's Passage: Read the *Gospel of John* for 20-30 minutes.**

Today continues your second (or third) journey through the *Gospel of John*. If everything is humming along for you, feel free to put this book down and just dive back into your reading.

But let me ask you: Are you up for a challenge?

If you'd like to add another "layer" to your journey, try listening to the *Gospel of John* between now and Day 11. Open up the YouVersion app or the Dwell app[1] and listen as you commute, walk the dog, do the dishes, or get ready for your day. It is amazing how many minutes we have in the day that we don't use intentionally.

Let's change that!

1. The Dwell app is a paid app, but it is amazing. They don't have as many translations as YouVersion, but they have multiple "voices" you can choose from, as well as different types of background music. You can even control the volume of the narrator and the music independently. Using my affiliate link – www.keithferrin.com/dwell - will give you a free trial.

## For Reflection & Discussion

- What stood out to you today as you read?
- What encouraged or challenged you?
- What confused you?
- What person or event are you looking forward to exploring more deeply?

## Notes & Prayers

# Day 9

**Today's Passage: Read the *Gospel of John* for 20-30 minutes and do a Background Study on the *Audience* and the *Atmosphere*.**

If you have a good study Bible, you probably have some of this info in your Bible. If not, there are many online resources available for free. You can simply search "free online study bible," or here are a couple of my favorites...

https://bible.faithlife.com/

https://www.blueletterbible.org/csb/jhn/1/1/t_comms_998001

Getting even a little background will be so helpful, not to mention making the reading more enjoyable! As with Day 5 (the day we did the *Author* background study), this can be 10-15 minutes, or might turn into an hour or two!

Many people don't think they're going to enjoy background studies. After giving it a try, they come to realize how much better they understand and relate to the Bible when they have more context to what they are reading. Give it a try!

## For Reflection & Discussion

- What stood out to you today as you read?
- What encouraged or challenged you?
- What confused you?
- What person or event are you looking forward to exploring more deeply?

## Notes & Prayers

# Day 10

**Today's Passage: Read the *Gospel of John* for 20-30 minutes.**

Today is our final "watch the play" day. Hopefully, you will be able to finish reading the *Gospel of John* today. If not, add on a day or two before diving into Day 11.

**Remember: This is your journey!**

Pushing yourself is good. Beating yourself up is not.

This is relational time. It's not about "getting through" the book. It's about hanging out with Jesus. Being in the presence of your Heavenly Father. Being guided by the Holy Spirit.

Reading the Bible *relationally* will always be better than simply reading *informationally*!

## For Reflection & Discussion

- What stood out to you today as you read?
- What encouraged or challenged you?
- What confused you?
- What person or event are you looking forward to exploring more deeply?
- Do you feel you know the personality and character of Jesus better after reading through the whole story?

## Notes & Prayers

# Day 11

## Today's Passage: Read *John 1:1-34*.

Today is the first day of "studying the scenes." We have "watched the play" a few times. You might want to bookmark this page because I am including some *General Questions* you can use every day. These questions are good ones to use anytime you are reading *any* Bible passage.

### General Questions (for every day)

- What does this passage say about who God is?
- What does this passage say about what God has done?
- What does this passage say about your identity?
- What encourages you?
- What challenges you?
- What questions do you have?
- How will you respond?

**NOTE: This last question is *not always* an "application point."** Sometimes your response is an application. Other days your response is to explore a question. Or worship. Or sit in silence. Or change a thought or attitude. Or pray and discuss the passage with God, a family member, or friend.

You have been used to reading for 20-30 minutes (or more) each day. Just because reading these sections will take you a fraction of that time, don't simply finish early. Soak in the passage. Ponder it. Pray through it. Read it in a couple different translations. Truly enter into this amazing story.

In these first 34 verses, John covers a lot of ground. In fact, he goes back all the way into...well...eternity past. Our minds can conceive eternity moving forward. But not eternity past.

This word – The Word – was "*in the beginning.*" He was before time. He was beyond time. And yet, He entered the very time, space, and physicality He had created.

Why? To shine light in the darkness.

The Light created the world. The Light came into the world. John the Baptist bore witness to the Light. So do you and I.

## For Reflection & Discussion

- Ponder the unfathomableness of the incarnation. Let it lead you to worship.
- When you think of "eternity past" and "eternity future," what thoughts and images do you have?
- Verse 18 says, "*No one has ever seen God, but the one and only Son, who is Himself God and is at the Father's side, has made Him known.*" Spend some time asking Jesus to show you the Father as you get to know Him better through this journey.
- How might you reflect the Light to those around you?

## Notes & Prayers

# Day 12

**Today's Passage: Read *John 1:35-51*.**

There are two important concepts woven throughout today's reading. Following and inviting.

Andrew and another disciple were following John the Baptist. When John told them who Jesus was, they followed Jesus. When Jesus invited them to *"Come and see,"* they followed Him.

When Andrew invited Peter to come see Jesus, Peter followed his brother. When Jesus gave Peter a new name – and invited him into a new life – Peter followed Him for the rest of his life! (We know this from the remainder of this gospel and the book of *Acts*.)

When Jesus invited Philip to follow Him, he did exactly that. When Philip invited Nathanael to *"Come and see,"* Nathanael followed Philip. When Jesus invited Nathanael on a journey where he *"will see even greater things than these,"* Nathanael followed Jesus.

Invite. Follow. Invite. Follow. Invite.

This passage shows us that bringing people to Jesus (what many refer to as "evangelism") doesn't have to be complicated. In fact, it's much more effective when we keep it simple.

## For Reflection & Discussion

- Which is more natural for you – following or inviting?
- How is Jesus inviting you to follow Him right now?
- Who does Jesus want you to invite to *"Come and see"*?

## Notes & Prayers

# DAY 13

**Today's Passage: Read *John 2:1-25.***

Today you will read two of the most famous events in the life of Jesus. Simply saying, "water to wine" or "Jesus overturns tables" will typically get the type of head nod and grin that comes with familiarity.

As you read these familiar events, take notice of three truths that are foundational as you read the rest of John's gospel (and the rest of the Bible for that matter).

Truth 1: Jesus begins from a place of abundance. This is Jesus's first miracle. What does He do? He turns water into wine (fine wine at that!) so that a celebration could continue. (Check out John 10:10 if you want to hear more from Jesus about abundance.)

Truth 2: Jesus notices you. As you were reading, did you catch Verse 9?

> *"He [the master of the banquet] did not know where it was from, but the servants who had drawn the water knew."*

Nobody noticed the servants. They weren't supposed to notice the servants. The servants were supposed to do their jobs and remain invisible. But not to Jesus. Jesus noticed them. Not only did He notice them, He let them in on the secret of His first miracle. When you feel "unnoticed," Jesus notices you.

Truth 3: Jesus will do anything to remove the barriers between you and His Father. At the place of worship, the people who should be ushering others into the Father's presence put up barriers instead. Conditions. Requirements. And Jesus would have none of it. He overturned the tables and removed the barriers.

Ultimately, an empty cross and an empty tomb will remove the barriers for good!

## For Reflection & Discussion

- Which of these truths most resonate with you today?
- Is your mindset (toward yourself and others) one of "lack" or "abundance"?
- How does it feel to know that Jesus notices you?
- Are there any barriers in your own life that Jesus has removed, but you continue to rebuild?

## Notes & Prayers

# Day 14

**Today's Passage: Read *John 3:1-21*.**

Yesterday's reading contained two of the most famous events in the life of Jesus. In today's reading, we find the most famous *verse* in the entire Bible. Most people can quote John 3:16 without even thinking. (That's part of the problem.)

But did you ever think about the context of that verse? These words weren't spoken on a mountainside with thousands of listeners. They weren't spoken over a meal with Jesus's close disciples. He didn't shout them from the cross (when He was living out the truth of the words).

He spoke these words in a conversation, late at night, with one person. Nicodemus had knowledge. He also had questions. He was likely scared of what people thought. (Thus, the nighttime visit.) He was confused by some of what Jesus said. He had a hard time marrying what he thought he believed, long-standing tradition, and what Jesus was now saying.

Jesus spoke of God's love for the whole world. And yet, He spoke these words to one person.

Jesus didn't just come for "everyone." Jesus came for "each" one. Even you.

## For Reflection & Discussion

- When do you first remember hearing John 3:16?
- How does it inform your thinking that Jesus came for each one (not just everyone)?
- What else from Jesus's conversation with Nicodemus stands out to you?
- Spend some time re-reading and praying through the final sentences about "light and darkness." What comes to mind as you think about light and darkness (in the world and in your own life)?

## Notes & Prayers

# Day 15

**Today's Passage: Read *John 3:22-36.***

John the Baptist models humble deflection. He doesn't say he is worthless. He doesn't downplay his calling. In fact, he boldly enters into his calling. And his calling is our calling – to point people to Jesus.

John could say, *"He must increase; I must decrease"* because he knew three things for certain.

He knew that Jesus was the bridegroom. He knew the church was the bride. And he knew that he was the friend of the bridegroom.

Is the "best man" important at a wedding? For sure. That said, if the best man is bringing attention to himself, something is wildly amiss. The best man's mission is to make sure the bride and the bridegroom are the focus. Their relationship. Their joy. Their union.

Jesus must always increase. You and I – when we decrease – are doing exactly what we're supposed to do.

## For Reflection & Discussion

- What inspires or challenges you about John the Baptist's example?
- How might you help Jesus "increase" to those around you? (e.g. family, work, school, neighborhood, etc.)
- In what ways do you need to "decrease?"

## Notes & Prayers

# Day 16

For the next several days, you will be reading a full chapter each day. There are so many encounters, conversations and events, that it would be very easy to make each day into 3-4 days. (I figured a *100-Day Scripture Journey* would be a little daunting!)

I will typically pick one element of each chapter to focus on. But remember, this is *your* journey.

You might choose to focus your praying, journaling and pondering on the section I write about, or you might focus on something else entirely. Since each chapter only takes a few minutes to read, you could read it a few different times throughout your day, centering your attention on a different person, event or truth from the chapter.

## Today's Passage: Read *John 4:1-54.*

So many aspects of Jesus's interaction with the Samaritan woman are amazing. The first is that Jesus, a Jewish man, speaks to a Samaritan woman at all. She is "unclean." And yet, He asks her for a drink.

Then He speaks to her – with compassion and truth. She asks questions. He answers. Truthfully and compassionately. She's not used to people talking to her this way. In fact, she experiences compassion so rarely, she would rather come to the well in the middle of the day, when the sun is strongest, but the chance of seeing other people is at its lowest.

What is the result of truth combined with compassion? Transformation.

She was transformed from a people-avoider to a people-pursuer. The very people she spent years avoiding are the ones she now seeks out, tells her story to, and brings to Jesus.

The result? More transformation. Transformed by her story. (Verse 39). Transformed by Jesus's words. (Verse 41.)

Combining truth and compassion is always transformative.

## For Reflection & Discussion

- What part of her story do you most relate to? (Sin, shame, transformation, questioning, etc.)
- When the disciples return, they all but ignore the woman. Are you ever tempted to ignore people Jesus values?
- Some of the Samaritans believed because of the woman's story. Others because of Jesus's words. Who were the first people who led you to believe in Jesus?
- Verse 50 tells us that the royal official *"took Jesus at His word and departed."* Have you ever "taken Jesus at His word" and trusted Him to act?

## Notes & Prayers

# Day 17

**Today's Passage: Read *John 5:1-47*.**

In the middle of today's reading – Verse 18 – is the first time we read of the Jews wanting to kill Jesus. Why? The rest of the verse gives us the answer...

> *"Because of this, the Jews tried all the harder to kill Him. Not only was He breaking the Sabbath, but He was even calling God His own Father, making Himself equal with God."*

Everything in this chapter (and the entire *Gospel of John*) testifies that Jesus is God.

At the beginning of this chapter, we see Jesus impart divine healing to someone who hadn't walked in nearly four decades. These "works" testify about Jesus. Jesus testifies about Himself. John the Baptist testified about Jesus. The Father Himself testifies about Jesus. The words of Scripture testify about Jesus.

It's important to note that when Jesus says – Verse 39 – "*These are the very words that testify about Me*" He is speaking of the Old Testament. We read the word "Scripture," and we think "Old and New Testament." But when Jesus said this, the only "Scripture" was what we now call the Old Testament. Yes! Even the Old Testament points to Jesus!

The works. John the Baptist. Jesus Himself. The Father. The Scriptures. All of these testify to the only One who can save. Maybe you and I should testify to the One who saves as well.

## For Reflection & Discussion

- How could you "testify" about Jesus?
- What causes you to believe in Jesus?
- How do you see Jesus in the Old Testament?
- What has Jesus ever "healed" in you? (Physical, emotional, spiritual, relational, mental, etc.)

## Notes & Prayers

# Day 18

**Today's Passage: Read *John 6:1-71*.**

This chapter has four different accounts. Each of them begs the question, "*Are we focusing on Jesus, or something else?*"

In the first, Philip is focused on the vast crowd and Andrew is focused on the tiny lunch. The young boy is focused on Jesus, and over 5,000 people are fed.

In the second, the disciples are focused on the storm, the "ghost," and their own fears. And yet, only Jesus can calm the storm...and our fears.

Then we see a crowd focused on seeing miracles and the absurdity of Jesus's words about eating flesh and drinking blood. Jesus is focused on offering them life through faith.

Finally, we see some turn away as they are focused on the difficulty of Jesus's words. Peter, however, is focused on Jesus Himself, realizing that focusing on Jesus – no matter how difficult – is the only way to live. After all, Jesus is the only one who has "*the words of eternal life.*"

## For Reflection & Discussion

- What big problem (vast crowd) or perceived lack (tiny lunch) are you tempted to focus on right now?
- What storm are you focusing on? How could you shift your focus to the One who calms the storm?
- Are you tempted to need "one more sign?" Spend some time looking back at all the ways Jesus has already shown up in your life.
- How do you respond to Jesus's question, "*Do you want to leave too?*"

## Notes & Prayers

# Day 19

**Today's Passage: Read *John 7:1-52.***

This chapter covers about as wide a range of responses to Jesus as you'll see in one chapter. Imagine Jesus's heartbreak as His own brothers mock Him in unbelief. The unbelief of the brothers is just one response.

There is also the curiosity of the people attending the feast. The respect of some in the crowd who spoke of Jesus being "*a good man.*" The doubt of others who retorted, "*No, He deceives the people.*" The fear of those who wouldn't say anything publicly. The amazement of some as they heard Jesus teach. The accusation of those who said Jesus had a demon. The anger of those who wanted him arrested. The faith of some who finally believed. The pride of those who saw their status and power threatened. The boldness of the officers who refused to arrest Jesus. The growing faith of Nicodemus. (The same guy who visited Jesus "at night" a few chapters back and now speaks on Jesus's behalf in the presence of his fellow Pharisees and the chief priests).

Mocking. Curiosity. Respect. Doubt. Amazement. Accusation. Anger. Faith. Pride. Boldness. Growing Faith.

Sounds pretty similar to the varied responses to Jesus we see today.

## For Reflection & Discussion

- Have you ever struggled with doubt or mocking from family members (or those close to you)?
- Which of these "responses" to Jesus have you had in the past?
- Which of these "responses" are you currently having?
- Have you ever stood up for Jesus? Did it cost you something (the way it did for Nicodemus)?

## Notes & Prayers

# Day 20

**Today's Passage: Read *John 8:1-59.***

Each of the four "scenes" in this chapter is very popular. After all, are there any of these you *don't* recognize when I say a simple phrase?

- Woman Caught in Adultery
- Jesus is the Light of the World
- The Truth Will Set You Free
- "I Am"

You might want to pause and ponder after each section. Or you might pick one section and soak in it for the day. Or you might do four shorter readings spread throughout your day.

However you choose to meditate on today's reading, I pray this truth over you...

> *"May the great I Am – the One who has existed since before time began, the one who is the Truth that sets you free, the One who is the Light of the World that never dims – May you remember that He stands beside you. Even when everyone else wants to throw stones. Amen."*

## For Reflection & Discussion

- How might you stand next to someone when others want to throw stones? Is there a specific person or situation that comes to mind today?
- Where do you need the Light of the World to light up a dark area of your life?
- How has the Truth set you free?
- What does it mean to you that Jesus is the “I Am” that has always been and always will be?

## Notes & Prayers

# Day 21

**Today's Passage: Read *John 9:1-41*.**

What if the best day of your life was also one of the worst? I wonder if that's how the blind man felt after receiving his sight.

His day starts out with Jesus and the disciples talking about sin and the reason for his blindness. Then Jesus puts spit-mud on his eyes and tells him to go wash it off. (Hmm...Was there another option?!) He does. And he sees! Best. Day. Ever!

Did you notice how badly *everything* went after that?

His neighbors didn't believe he was the same guy. The religious people were, at first, concerned about religious rules. Then they simply didn't believe the man had ever been blind in the first place.

The real tragedy comes when the religious leaders bring his parents in. We don't know for sure, but this might just be the very first time in his life that he's seeing his parents. Instead of celebrating with him they distance themselves from him.

This poor man must have been confused at best and devastated at worst. And yet, through it all, his story is the same.

*"Jesus touched me. I can see now."*

He didn't have all the answers. And you don't need to either. Whether you are celebrating, confused, or devasted, your responsibility is to share the difference Jesus has made in your life. And when you stand face-to-face with Jesus, do what this guy did – worship.

## For Reflection & Discussion

- I'm sure spit-and-dirt isn't how this guy would have scripted his healing. How has Jesus shown up in your life in different ways than you expected (or wanted)?
- When have you been disappointed by someone else's response to God's working in your life?
- How have you dealt with confusion, disappointment, or devastation in your life?
- How might you worship Jesus in the midst of the celebration and the challenge?

## Notes & Prayers

# Day 22

**Today's Passage: Read *John 10:1-42*.**

Other than John 3:16, John 10:10 might be the most famous verse in John's gospel.

> *"The thief comes only to steal and kill and destroy. I have come that they may have life, and have it in all its fullness."*

That statement begs the question, "How do we experience the 'life in all its fullness' Jesus offers?"

The answer comes as we look at the rest of the conversation. Four times in Jesus's next few sentences He uses the word "know."

He speaks of Himself (the Good Shepherd) knowing the sheep and the sheep knowing Him. He also speaks of Himself knowing the Father and the Father knowing Him.

The Greek word Jesus uses here is "ginosko." Ginosko is a *relational* type of knowing, not an *informational* type. It is an *intimate* type of knowing, not an *intellectual* type.

If you want life in all its fullness, there's only one way to get it. Develop a deep, personal, intimate, ever-growing, day-by-day relationship with Jesus – your Good Shepherd.

## For Reflection & Discussion

- How have you grown in your ability to recognize the voice of the Good Shepherd?
- What is one step you can take to deepen your relationship with Jesus?
- What stood out to you from Jesus's interaction with the people at the Feast of Dedication?
- What contributed to you putting your faith in Jesus (like those mentioned in verses 40-42)?

## Notes & Prayers

# Day 23

**Today's Passage: Read *John 11:1-44.***

Have you ever noticed that Martha and Mary, Lazarus's two sisters, both said the exact same thing as soon as they saw Jesus?

*"Lord, if You had been here, my brother would not have died."* (Verses 21 and 32)

And yet, Jesus's response to each sister is completely different. With Martha, Jesus goes into explanations about rising again, believing, dying, and never dying again. He even asks her if she believes.

With Mary, he weeps.

Both lost their brother. Both went to Jesus. Both said the same thing.

Jesus met them where they were. And He met them in the way that they needed Him.

Jesus will meet you where you are. In exactly the way that you need Him to.

## For Reflection & Discussion

- How do Jesus's "personalized" responses encourage you?
- Do you go to Jesus with your questions...and your grief?
- We don't have a record of it, but imagine the first post-tomb conversation between Lazarus and Jesus!
- What thoughts and questions do you have as you read of the plot to kill Jesus at the end of this chapter?

## Notes & Prayers

# DAY 24

**Today's Passage: Read *John 11:45-12:11*.**

Give yourself permission to go on the roller coaster ride of events and emotions today. In 24 verses we see a plot to kill Jesus, followed by Jesus retreating away from Jerusalem to Ephraim, and crowds searching for Jesus back in Jerusalem at the Passover Feast.

We see a dinner in which one of the hosts is Lazarus, who had recently spent four days in a tomb! Martha serves the people. Mary anoints Jesus's feet. Judas Iscariot begins to display his displeasure...that will soon lead to betrayal. Finally, we see a plot to kill Lazarus as well. After all, coming back from the dead is a pretty strong testimony that the chief priests wanted to silence.

Love. Betrayal. Power. Pride. Community. Celebration. Confusion. Searching. Let your thoughts and emotions journey with the One who walks your multi-faceted journey with you.

## For Reflection & Discussion

- Had you ever noticed that the chief priests wanted to kill Lazarus as well?
- Which of the events and emotions did you find yourself lingering on today?
- How does it impact you that Jesus experienced such a wide range of experiences and emotions (just like you)?

## Notes & Prayers

# Day 25

**Today's Passage: Read *John 12:12-50.***

Yesterday had a variety of events and emotions. Today has a variety of *responses* to Jesus. One thing I love about this chapter is that it has all types of people responding in all types of ways. We don't have one group that "gets it" and another that doesn't.

Early on we see the people who had come for the feast (the everyday Jews) worshipping Jesus as the Messiah. In verse 16, the disciples are confused. A couple verses later, "many people" testify that they had been there for the raising of Lazarus.

The Greeks (outsiders to those gathering for the Passover Feast) approach a couple disciples to seek out a personal visit with Jesus. When Jesus speaks – followed by the Father's thunderous voice from heaven – some believe and some don't. Verse 42 reminds us that some of the people who believed were among the religious leaders.

Jesus knew that all kinds of people would have all kinds of responses to Him. He also knew that His focus needed to be less about judgment and more about speaking "*exactly what the Father has told Me to say.*" Maybe you and I should do the same.

## For Reflection & Discussion

- Which of the responses to Jesus do you most relate to in this chapter?
- How do you respond when others respond in different ways to Jesus?
- In verse 26 we see a call to serve Jesus, follow Jesus, and be with Jesus. What is one step you can take today in response to each?
- Is there anything the Father is telling you to say that you're not saying?

## Notes & Prayers

# Day 26

**Today's Passage: Read *John 13:1-38*.**

We learn a lot about love in today's reading. The very first verse introduces the famous "Last Supper" scene. John sets the stage this way...

> *"Having loved His own who were in the world, He loved them to the very end."*

Footnotes in many Bibles explain that the phrase "*loved them to the very end*" could also be translated "*showed them the full extent of His love.*" We see His love on full display in the paragraphs that follow.

Jesus washes feet. Many authors, speakers, and pastors have pointed out the amazing love Jesus showed by washing the feet of Judas Iscariot, whom Jesus knew was only hours away from betraying Him.

But what about the rest of them? In Matthew's gospel, he includes a detail that provides some important context. Matthew 26 is where we find the betrayal by Judas and the arrest of Jesus. Look at verse 56...

> *"Then **all** the disciples deserted Him and fled."* (emphasis added)

One of the twelve would blatantly betray Him. One of them would deny Him three times. All of them would desert Him. Jesus knew it, and He still washed their feet. And then He commands them to love each other, reminding them that "*everyone will know that you are My disciples, if you love one another.*"

Love spoken. Love demonstrated. Love commanded. And in a few days, He will show that love...to the very end.

## For Reflection & Discussion

- How does today's reading inform your view of love?
- Can you imagine Jesus washing your feet?
- Would people around you know you are a disciple of Jesus by the way you love others?

## Notes & Prayers

# Day 27

**Today's Passage: Read *John 14:1-31*.**

Let's look at four words today. Way. Truth. Life. Peace.

Way – You only need to know the way if there's a place to go. Jesus not only points out that He's the Way, but He reminds us of where we're going. To a room, prepared for you, in His Father's House.

Truth – Truth is needed when the lies are loud. Jesus speaks of the Spirit of truth, who will be with us forever. In verse 26, we see that the reason the Advocate – the Holy Spirit – is being sent is to "*teach you all things and remind you*." We not only need to know the truth. We also need to be reminded of the truth.

Life – Speaking of reminders, do you remember what Jesus said about the reason He came? "*That they may have life, and have it in all its fullness.*" Later on, in John 20:31, we'll read that John's primary purpose for writing his Gospel is "*that by believing you may have life in His name.*"

Peace – Oh, how we long for peace! Jesus not only *is* the way, the truth, and the life. He is also the only One who *can* offer peace. Not just temporary, circumstantial peace. His way-making, truth-telling, life-giving peace.

## For Reflection & Discussion

- What do you envision when you think of Jesus preparing a place for you in the Father's house?
- What are the lies you're tempted to believe? What is the truth the Holy Spirit is trying to remind you of today?
- Spend some time thanking Jesus for the life He offers you.
- Where do you need Jesus's peace in your life? Spend some time talking to Him about it...and receiving the peace He offers you.

## Notes & Prayers

# Day 28

**Today's Passage: Read *John 15:1-16:33*.**

Today's reading is the longest in the Gospel of John Scripture Journey. Two full chapters. This is the final conversation Jesus is having with His disciples before He prays in the garden and is betrayed by Judas and arrested. An entire book could be written (and several have been) based on the words you'll read today.

As you read many words today, let one word be the background music.

> *"Remain"*

Jesus uses the word *remain* twelve times in the first several paragraphs. Some translations use the word *abide* or *continue* or *dwell.*

The Greek word (meno) used for "remain" carries at least three characteristics. First, a "meno" type of remaining is intimate. Second, meno is permanent. Third, meno is fruitful.

An intimate, permanent, fruitful relationship with Jesus. That's a relationship worth remaining in!

## For Reflection & Discussion

- What is one practical way you can remain (abide, continue, dwell) in Christ?
- How might you grow in your intimacy with Jesus?
- How does it make you feel to know that Jesus is calling you to a permanent relationship with Him?
- Where is your relationship with Jesus resulting in fruitfulness? How could you grow in fruitfulness?

## Notes & Prayers

# Day 29

**Today's Passage: Read *John 17:1-26.***

If you've ever wanted a fly-on-the-wall view of a conversation between God the Father and Jesus the Son, today you're in luck. All but the first half of the first verse is Jesus speaking to His Father.

I highly recommend you read this prayer four times today. Each time, keep an eye out for one of the major themes woven throughout Jesus's prayer.

Glory – Past glory. Future glory. A reminder of glory. A request for glory. A gift of glory.

Unity – Unity between Father and Son. Unity between believers. Unity between the believers and Jesus.

Eternal Life – The definition of eternal life. The gift of eternal life.

Relationship – The relationship between Jesus and the disciples. Between Jesus and the Father. Between believers. Between us today.

If I had to describe this chapter in two words I would choose "intimate" and "beautiful."

Read it. Meditate on it. Enjoy it. Live it.

## For Reflection & Discussion

- What are your thoughts as you read this the first time? The second?
- What emotions do you see in Jesus as He prays?
- Which of the four themes struck you most today?
- What parts of Jesus's prayer do you need to turn into words you pray?

## Notes & Prayers

# Day 30

**Today's Passage: Read *John 18:1-40.***

This one chapter covers an evening, a night, and continues into the next morning (at least). As you witness each encounter and listen to each conversation, keep these words from the beginning of Verse 4 running in the background of your mind...

> *"Jesus, knowing all that was coming upon Him..."*

He knew the arrest – due to the betrayal by one of his best friends – was coming.

He knew Simon Peter would draw a sword to defend Him...and then deny Him.

He knew the verbal and physical assaults were coming.

He knew Pilate would question Him, attempt to release Him, have Him beaten, and finally turn Him over for crucifixion.

He knew the choice to free Barabbas was coming.

And yet, as Verse 4 continues, *"...[Jesus] stepped forward..."*

He stepped forward, toward it all, knowing what was coming.

And why did He step forward? The answer is in your mirror.

## For Reflection & Discussion

- Have you ever experienced a day that got harder and harder as each hour passed? How did you "step forward?"
- Pause after each encounter or conversation and jot down a word, phrase, or paragraph about what thoughts, questions, and emotions you have.
- Have you ever been like Peter, denying or distancing yourself from a friend or family member? Why? How did you respond? Is there any forgiveness you still need to request?
- The crowd chose Barabbas instead of Jesus. Have you ever "gone along with the crowd" and lived to regret it? What did you learn?

## Notes & Prayers

# Day 31

**Today's Passage: Read *John 19:1-16.***

Today and tomorrow will be very uncomfortable. And it should be. In a culture obsessed with comfort, the beating, mocking and crucifixion of the Creator of the Universe should have you cringing and more than a little sick to your stomach.

After all, it was brutal. It was messy. It was unjust. It was horrific. It was wrong.

Of course, sin is brutal, messy, unjust (against a holy God), horrific and wrong.

Why would we ever imagine that the solution to something so terrible would be comfortable?

It wasn't comfortable for Jesus. It shouldn't be comfortable for you and me either. Read slowly – and uncomfortably – today and tomorrow.

## For Reflection & Discussion

- Are you ever tempted to read the accounts of Jesus's arrest, beating, and crucifixion quickly?
- What do you imagine Jesus was thinking as He was beaten, questioned, and "gave no answer" (Verse 9)?
- In Verse 11, Jesus focuses on the One who actually has authority in this situation. How might you do the same the next time you are misjudged or mistreated?
- Imagine hearing the words *"Crucify Him!"* from the very ones you loved enough to die for. Let it lead you to a time of confession.

## Notes & Prayers

# DAY 32

**Today's Passage: Read *John 19:17-42.***

Today we continue the slow, uncomfortable journey from yesterday. The mocking. The tortuous pain that accompanied crucifixion. The emotional pain of seeing His mother and dear friend John (the author of this gospel) witnessing His death. The unfathomable – and never-before-experienced – pain of being separated from the other two members of the Trinity.

Let me remind you of Jesus's words from a few days ago...

> *"Jesus, knowing all that was coming upon Him, stepped forward..."*

Yes, Jesus knew the physical, emotional, and relational pain was coming. And yes, Jesus knew the cross was coming. Do you know what else He knew was coming? These words...

> *"It is finished."*

The cross was the only way. The only way to deal with sin. The only way to make your heart clean. The only way to make an eternal relationship between God and you possible.

In Jesus's eyes, you were worth dying for.

## For Reflection & Discussion

- Are you giving yourself permission to *not* be comfortable?
- When you think of physical, emotional, and relational pain, which is the hardest for you? How have you dealt with each?
- Meditate on the words *"It is finished."* Is there anything Jesus declares to be "finished" that you're still holding onto?
- Imagine the transformation that had to happen for Nicodemus – a Pharisee – to participate in the burial of Jesus and pay a wildly extravagant amount for the burial. What transformation have you seen in your own heart and mind when it comes to your faith in Jesus?

## Notes & Prayers

# Day 33

**Today's Passage: Read *John 20:1-18*.**

Today you will read about the most amazing event in human history. Death defeated. The grave conquered. The Savior risen!

Before you read, I want you to take a moment and ponder something that most of us never notice. Between the final word of Chapter 19 and the opening word of Chapter 20, there's an entire day.

I refer to it as *The Most Confusing Day in History.*

Before you walk, weep, and worship with Mary Magdalene. Before you run, reach the tomb, and return home with Peter and John. Before you declare, "He is risen!" remember Saturday.

Mary, Peter, and John had all watched Jesus die. Their Messiah. The One they followed. The One they trusted. The One they believed would conquer Rome and rule forever.

Jesus was dead. And they were confused and crushed.

They didn't understand Jesus's ways or His timing. All too often, neither do we. And yet, we go to the empty tomb and are reminded once again. He understands our confusion. He knows. He sees. He returns. He lives. He stays. He is risen! Indeed!

## For Reflection & Discussion

- Have you ever pondered the confusion of "Easter Saturday?"
- What do you think Mary believed she would find at the tomb?
- Why would John have stopped at the tomb's entrance? Why would Peter have rushed right in? Which would you have done?
- Spend some time thanking Jesus for His conquering of death and grave!

## Notes & Prayers

# DAY 34

**Today's Passage: Read *John 20:19-31*.**

Thomas gets a bad rap. When it comes to nicknames, I haven't heard of many worse than "Doubting Thomas." And this didn't last only through Middle School. This has been Thomas's nickname for two millennia!

Why? Because he wanted to see Jesus's hands and touch his side.

Did you notice what had happened eight days earlier? Thomas wasn't there. The other disciples were together and Jesus showed up. The first thing Jesus did was to say, *"Peace be with you!"* And the second thing is this...

> *"After He had said this, He showed them His hands and His side."* (Verse 20)

Then...

> *"The disciples rejoiced..."* (Verse 21)

Fast forward eight days. Jesus shows up. The first thing He does is say *"Peace be with you."* The second thing Jesus does is show Thomas *exactly what He had shown the others.* And Thomas rejoiced.

Jesus still shows up. Jesus still offers peace. Jesus still shows us His scars. And we still believe and rejoice.

## For Reflection & Discussion

- What nicknames (for yourself, family members, or friends) do you remember the most?
- We identify Thomas by his doubt. Jesus identified him by his belief. What "identity" are you carrying that Jesus wants you to exchange for something truer?
- We all have scars. Including Jesus. In what ways does this truth encourage you?
- John states his purpose for writing in Verse 31: *"But these are written so that you may believe that Jesus is the Christ, the Son of God, and that by believing you may have life in His name."* Spend some time pondering – and thanking Jesus for – the situations, relationships, and "signs" that led you to believe.

## Notes & Prayers

# Day 35

**Today's Passage: Read *John 21:1-25*.**

Have you ever wondered why Jesus did this particular miracle? I have.

It's not His "best" miracle. (After all, not too long ago, He had conquered death!) It's not to teach a lesson to a large crowd. (There are only seven people who witnessed it.) It's not to convince someone to believe. (All seven were disciples, and they had already seen Him since His resurrection.)

So, why did He do it?

I am sure there are some biblical scholars who might disagree with me, but I think Jesus did it because it was fun.

John points out an interesting detail. In Verse 4, he writes, *"...Jesus stood on the shore, but the disciples did not recognize that it was Jesus."* Practical jokes are best played when you know who and where your friends are, but they don't even know it's you!

Jesus had already taught them. Jesus had already led them. Jesus had already *"loved them to the very end."* (Remember John 13:1?) Later on, he will *remind* Peter of how much He loves him.

But for now, He takes this moment to show them that He *likes* them. He jokes with them. He invites them to join Him for a meal. He cooks for them.

Does Jesus love you? Without a doubt. But as you read today, let this story remind you that Jesus also *likes* you.

## For Reflection & Discussion

- Have you ever witnessed something miraculous? Let that memory feed your faith.
- Why do *you* think Jesus did this miracle?
- Have you ever thought about Jesus not only loving you, but liking you? What impact does that have on you?
- What stands out to you about the conversation Jesus had with Peter?

## Notes & Prayers

# Day 36

## Today's Passage: Read the *Gospel of John* for 20-30 minutes.

These final five days, we will once again focus on "watching the play." The goal is to read through the *Gospel of John* once or twice this week. You might even want to read it in one translation and use your commute, chores, or exercise time to *listen* to it in a different translation.

However you choose to do it, here's the goal: Enjoy the read!

## For Reflection & Discussion

For the next several days, the questions will be the same each day.

- What stood out to you today that you missed the last time you read it?
- What is something you want to study more deeply when the *Gospel of John Scripture Journey* comes to an end?
- What is your response to today's reading? (Application? Worship? Prayer? Awe?)

## Notes & Prayers

# Day 37

## Today's Passage: Read the *Gospel of John* for 20-30 minutes.

For today's reading, pick a *person* (or group of people) to focus your attention on. Enter into their story. Imagine their thoughts and emotions.

Learn from them. Be encouraged by them. Be challenged by them. Be comforted by their words or actions.

Sometimes, especially if you're reading a familiar passage, reading it through the lens of a single person in the account can open your eyes to elements you haven't noticed before. (We'll do something similar for the next few days.)

## For Reflection & Discussion

- What stood out to you today that you missed the last time you read it?
- What is something you want to study more deeply when the *Gospel of John Scripture Journey* comes to an end?
- What is your response to today's reading? (Application? Worship? Prayer? Awe?)

## Notes & Prayers

# Day 38

**Today's Passage: Read the *Gospel of John* for 20-30 minutes.**

As with yesterday, we're going to read a lot, but focus on something specific. Today, let your focus land on one of the "teachings" of Jesus.

Every single chapter has Jesus speaking and teaching. If you happen to have a "red letter" edition of the Bible (where the words of Jesus are in red ink), you'll see that the percentage of red letters in the *Gospel of John* is higher than in any of the other three gospels. In fact, there isn't an all-black-ink chapter in the whole book!

Begin by praying that God would show you which "teaching" of Jesus to focus on. If you're reading 3-5 chapters, there will be a lot to choose from.

Once you land on one, read it slowly. Jot down what stands out to you, encourages you, challenges you, or confuses you.

## Reflection & Discussion

- What stood out to you today that you missed the last time you read it?
- What is something you want to study more deeply when the *Gospel of John Scripture Journey* comes to an end?
- What is your response to today's reading? (Application? Worship? Prayer? Awe?)

## Notes & Prayers

# Day 39

**Today's Passage: Read the *Gospel of John* for 20-30 minutes.**

The last couple days we have focused on a *person* and then a *teaching*. Today, focus on a single *event*. You might read through dozens of them in your Bible time today. Certainly jot down any themes, recurring messages, or parts you want to study more deeply in the days or weeks to come.

Then pick one event. Soak in it. Read it with *all* your senses. Don't only see it with your mind's eye. Hear the scene with your mind's ear. Smell the scene with your mind's nose. Taste the flavors (if food is involved) with your mind's mouth. And experience the feelings with your mind's touch.

This "full senses experience" is a good habit to get into with any narrative passage.

## For Reflection & Discussion

- What stood out to you today that you missed the last time you read it?
- What is something you want to study more deeply when the *Gospel of John Scripture Journey* comes to an end?
- What is your response to today's reading? (Application? Worship? Prayer? Awe?)

# Notes & Prayers

# Day 40

**Today's Passage: Read the *Gospel of John* for 20-30 minutes.**

John ends his book with these words...

*"There are many more things that Jesus did. If all of them were written down, I suppose that not even the world itself would have space for the books that would be written."*

One of the reasons that the world "would not have space" is that Jesus is still writing His story. He didn't just live, teach some things, do some things, and go back to Heaven.

He is still alive. He is still moving. He is still teaching. He is still acting. And one part of His story He is still writing...is yours.

Our journey in this amazing account by "*the one whom Jesus loved*" comes to an end today. Do not let *your* journey with the *Gospel of John* end today. I pray that you return to it again and again.

Several years from now, you can pull out this book and go on another 40-day journey. You can also use this simple concept – Watch the play. Explore the acts. Study the scenes. – to do a shorter or longer study of the *Gospel of John*.

As we finish, my prayer for you is ...

> *Lord Jesus, the Word who was, is, and will always be speaking. May You speak life, light, and love into these journey-goers' hearts, minds, and souls. May they know You as the their Shepherd, Savior, and Friend. May their faith grow more and more as they experience, each and every day, life...in all its fullness. Amen.*

Alongside,

Keith

## For Reflection & Discussion

- What stood out to you today that you missed the last time you read it?
- What is something you want to study more deeply when the *Gospel of John Scripture Journey* comes to an end?
- What is your response to today's reading? (Application? Worship? Prayer? Awe?)

## Notes & Prayers

# About the Author

Am I the only one who thinks it is a little bit strange that the "About the Author" page is typically the only page in an entire book written in the third person? After all, I am the author. I am writing this page. It feels a bit weird to write about myself in the third person.

So let's try this...

I, Keith Ferrin, am an author, speaker, storyteller, and messaging coach. My passion is helping individuals, families, and entire church communities move from "should" to "want" when it comes to reading the Bible. I believe the Bible isn't just true, but it's also awesome! When I'm not the one on stage, I'm typically helping coach the people who are. I love to help C-level leaders, teams, pastors and entrepreneurs simplify their messages and deliver them well.

Actually, I guess all that is more of what I "do." As far as who I am...I am a disciple of Jesus Christ, a husband to Kari (world's most outstanding wife), and a father to Sarah, Caleb, and Hannah (the three coolest – and craziest – kids on the planet).

In case you are still reading...I am also a coffee drinker, ice cream eater, amateur guitar player, lover of twisty-turny movies, and eater of almost any kind of food (except olives).

If you're looking for me, head on up to Seattle. I will be the happy guy hanging out with his wife and kids doing something outside. Unless, of course, it is family movie night. Then we'll be inside.

# A Few of My Other Books

## The Scripture Journey Series

**Acts Scripture Journey** – Take a journey through the first few decades of the early church. Jesus has walked the earth, died, and risen. *Acts* opens with Jesus's ascension into heaven. The Luke (the author) takes us first-hand through the first followers of Jesus, the lives of Peter, James, John, and the missionary journeys of the Apostle Paul. Read Reviews on Amazon

**Ephesians Scripture Journey** – When it comes to living out our faith, the temptation is to make it all about morality – doing the *right* things and avoiding the *wrong* things. In Paul's letter to the *Ephesians*, he takes a different approach altogether. Paul's letter to the Church in Ephesus will remind you of your identity in Christ, so you can live with greater freedom, boldness, authenticity, and purpose. Read Reviews on Amazon

**Colossians Scripture Journey** – Are you tempted to view "Bible times" as a culture we can't relate to today? Paul's letter to the church in Colossae shows us just how similar our culture is to theirs. Paul combines the knowledge of a theologian, the truth-telling of a good friend, and the heart of a parent to encourage his readers – and us – to not only believe in Jesus, but to grow each day in understanding, faith, and obedience.

**2 Timothy Scripture Journey** – What would you write if you were in prison, on Death Row, knowing you were experiencing your final days on earth, and you were writing a letter to someone you had mentored, who was now one of your best friends? That's exactly the situation Paul was in when he wrote 2

Timothy...his final letter. Paul writes about hardships and suffering. He writes about living out your calling. He writes about God's faithfulness. He writes about Christ's example. He writes about fleeing evil. He writes about pursuing good. And the list goes on and on.. Read Reviews on Amazon

**Hebrews Scripture Journey** – In this study, you will discover the significance of Christ as the ultimate High Priest, perfect sacrifice, and mediator of a new covenant. You will uncover the richness of God's redemptive plan, rooted in the Old Testament and fulfilled in Jesus. You will anchor your faith in unchanging promises, find the strength to run life's race, and embrace a life fully devoted to God. Read Reviews on Amazon

**1 Peter Scripture Journey** – Living out a life that honors Jesus is hard. Really hard. Our culture doesn't encourage it. In fact, in so many ways, it opposes it. Peter's first letter is filled with encouragement and guidance to help us walk the path of pursuing holiness in a world that pushes us to do the opposite. His call to live holy lives is surrounded by reminders of God's goodness, faithfulness, and never-ending presence. Read Reviews on Amazon

**Advent Scripture Journey** – Too often, the days and weeks leading up to Christmas Morning are filled with busyness. We're busy shopping. We're busy wrapping. We're busy cooking. We're busy with parties. We're busy with friends and family. This December, take a few minutes each day to go on a journey. A journey through the whole Bible, beginning on Page 1 and taking you to the manger. To pause. To remember. To reflect. To be fully present. To worship. Read Reviews on Amazon

**Lent Scripture Journey** – As you prepare for Easter, the *Lent Scripture Journey* will be your daily guide from Ash Wednesday through Easter Morning. While some Lenten devotionals focus only on the final week – from the Triumphal Entry to Resurrection Morning – the *Lent Scripture Journey* takes you through the full life of Jesus. After all, Jesus's birth, life, teaching, miracles, suffering and crucifixion were all pointing to the glory of the empty grave!. Read Reviews on Amazon

## How to Enjoy Reading Your Bible

Do you enjoy the Bible? If we enjoy the Bible, we will read it. If we enjoy it, we'll talk about it. If we enjoy it, consistency won't be a problem. After almost three decades of speaking and writing, I have compiled my "Top 10 Tips" for enjoying the Bible. Tips that are applicable immediately. Written using stories, analogies, and common language, these tips are equally accessible for someone who is exploring, is new to faith in Jesus, or has been hanging out with Jesus for decades. If you want to enjoy the Bible – I wrote this book for you. Because believing it's true is not enough. Read Reviews on Amazon

## Like Ice Cream: The Scoop on Helping the Next Generation Fall in Love with God's Word

What if passing on a love for God's Word could be as natural – and enjoyable – as passing on a love for ice cream? I believe it can be. When it comes to helping the next generation fall in love with the Bible, the principles are surprisingly similar to the way a love for ice cream gets passed on from generation to generation. Whether you are a parent, grandparent, youth pastor – or anyone who cares deeply about the next generation – you will find *Like Ice Cream* filled with encouragement and practical ideas you can start using today. Read Reviews on Amazon

## Falling in Love with God's Word

This book will help you discover what God always intended Bible study to be. God wants you to understand His Word. He wants you to enjoy your time in His Word. He wants you to remember what you read in His Word. In this book, I walk you through my entire process for deeply studying a book of the Bible. My prayer is this book will transform your Bible study time in a way that will allow God to use His Word to transform you! Read Reviews on Amazon

## Rapid Bible Read Thru

Have you ever read through the whole Bible? Have you ever started...only to stop after a few weeks? Do you wish you understood the Bible better? Do you long to know The Author more deeply? If so, *Rapid Bible Read Thru* is just what you need!

Is it a challenge? *Yes*. It is easier than most people think? *Absolutely*. Will it transform your understanding of the Bible and deeper your relationship with God? *No doubt!* This book will walk you step-by-step through the Why, What, and How of doing a *Rapid Bible Read Thru*. Read Reviews on Amazon

## Bible Praying for Parents

As parents, we want to pray for our kids. We know we should pray for them. And yet, our prayers often feel repetitive. So then, how do we know what to pray? How do we know we are covering every aspect of their lives (rather than only what's urgent at the moment)? The answer is *Bible Praying*. After all, when we pray God's Word, we pray God's will.

I wrote this book with my friend Judy Fetzer, who introduced me to praying the words of Scripture for our children. In this book we've turned 365 Bible passages (in 20+ categories) into prayer. We've also included a section of *Bible Blessings* straight from God's Word. Read Reviews on Amazon

# BIBLE TOOLBOX

*Bible Toolbox* is the world's first "Guided AI" tool specifically designed for Bible study. I co-created it with my friend CJ McDaniel, the founder and CEO of Adazing (a software company that creates writing and marketing tools and training for authors).

Think of it as the power of AI with "guard rails." Using the ease of drop-down menus and simple prompts, *Bible Toolbox* allows you to do never-before-possible research in a fraction of the time – and at a fraction of the cost of other software tools or books.

Whether you have a lot of experience with technology or none at all, *Bible Toolbox* will guide you each step of the way!

**Here are just a handful of things *Bible Toolbox* can do:**

- Historical & Cultural Context
- In-Depth Verse Analysis
- Word and Phrase Studies
- Character or Topical Studies
- Sermon Prep (Research and Brainstorming Analogies and Illustrations)
- Family Devotions
- Reading & Prayer Plans
- Historical & Cultural Context
- Application Points
- Built-In Tools for Churches (social media, job descriptions, video scripts, etc.)
- And heaps more!

**Visit www.keithferrin.com/bibletoolbox for a special discount since you purchased this book!**

# Let's Connect!

I love to connect with my readers. Truly. Shoot me an email. I'll write back.

While there are several ways we can connect, here are the two easiest to start with...

- Email: keith@keithferrin.com
- Blog: www.keithferrin.com

You can also find me using @KeithFerrin on pretty much any social media platform.

linkedin.com/in/keithferrin/

If you have a question or comment, please shoot me a note. Most of the videos I create on YouTube, books I write, or resources I create come from suggestions or questions I hear from my readers.

So…fire away. I'd love to hear from you.

Alongside,

Keith

Made in the USA
Columbia, SC
01 May 2024

34795884R00078